THE LEANING TOWER OF PISA

by Mary Beth Jarvis Clark

PUBLISHED BY

Capstone Press

Mankato, MN, U.S.A.

Distributed By

CP CHILDRENS PRESS®
CHICAGO

CIP
LIBRARY OF CONGRESS CATALOGING IN PUBLICATION DATA

J 726
22 cm.

Clark, Mary Beth Jarvis.
The Leaning Tower of Pisa / by Mary Beth Jarvis Clark.
p. cm.--(Inside story)
Summary: A knowledgeable Italian gentleman explains the construction and history of an Italian landmark, now 800 years old, to two American children.
ISBN 1-56065-031-1
1. Leaning Tower (Pisa, Italy)--Juvenile literature.
2. Architecture, Romanesque--Italy--Pisa--Juvenile literature.
3. Church architecture--Italy--Pisa--Juvenile literature. 4. Pisa (Italy)--Buildings, structures, etc.--Juvenile literature. [1. Leaning Tower (Pisa, Italy) 2. Pisa (Italy)--Buildings, structures, etc.]
I. Title II. Series: Inside story (Mankato, Minn.)
NA5621.P716J37 1989
726'.597--dc20   89-70874 CIP AC

PHOTO CREDITS

Art Resource: 4, (Gian Berto Vanni) 28
Italian Government Travel Office, 9, 14, 21, 36-37, 45

Designed by Nathan Y. Jarvis & Associates, Inc.

Capstone Press
Box 669, Mankato, MN, U.S.A. 56001

CONTENTS

The Leaning Tower of Pisa tilts more and more every year. It has tilted so much that you can't go inside. It isn't safe to climb the tower now. But it used to be safe. People from all over the world came to Pisa to climb the tower. Leslie and Ray climbed the tower once. It was quite an adventure.

 ## WAITING BELOW

Leslie heard a rumble coming from close by.

"What on earth is that noise?" she asked.

"It's my stomach," replied Ray. "I'm hungry. I thought Mom and Dad said they were taking us to get pizza."

Leslie laughed. "Mom and Dad told us we were going to see Pisa, not to eat pizza."

"Well, I could have sworn they said we

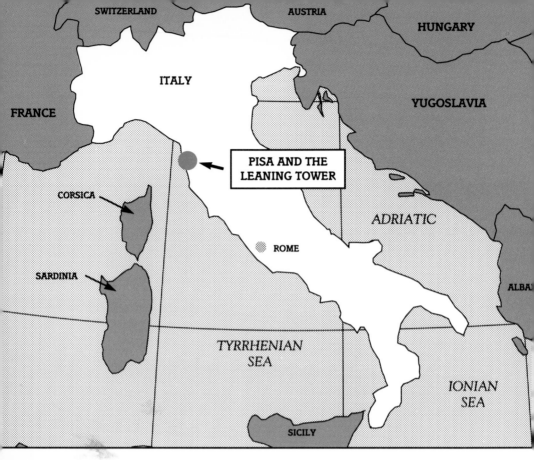

Italy, Pisa and the location of the Leaning Tower.

were going to get pizza," Ray said. "After all, we're in Italy. Pizza is Italian food, isn't it?"

Leslie rolled her eyes. "Pizza is Italian food. And Pisa is an Italian city."

"So what is there to do in Pisa?" Ray asked.

"Mom and Dad are inside the **cathedral** looking at the sculptures and paintings . . ." Ray sighed.

6

"But they said that their friend Signor Garibaldi would show us around the Leaning Tower of Pisa. Come on." She marched off across the big, green lawn. Ray followed her.

"Here it is," she said as they came to a stop in front of a tall, cylindrical building. "Signor Garibaldi should be here any minute."

Ray and Leslie stared up at the tilting tower in front of them.

"So what's so fun about the Leaning Tower of Pisa?" Ray asked.

"We can go inside it and climb all the way to the top," Leslie replied. "I'll bet it will be lots of fun."

"I don't know about this, Leslie." Ray crinkled his nose and squinted to get a better view of the tower's top. "It looks like it might come crashing down at any minute. In fact, I think we'd better get out of the way right now."

"I'm sure it's perfectly safe," Leslie said.

"She is right, you know. There is nothing to fear." A man in a white suit had come up to them. He bowed and took off his hat. "Allow me to introduce myself. My name is Signor Garibaldi, and you must be Leslie and Ray. Welcome to the Leaning Tower of Pisa."

THE SQUARE OF MIRACLES

Signor Garibaldi stopped at the entrance to the tower.

"Here in Italy, our name for the Leaning Tower is the Torre Pendente. As you know, the tower is part of a group of beautiful old buildings. First comes the **baptistery**, which we call the Battistero. Then comes the cathedral, which we call the Duomo. Next to the cathedral is the enclosed cemetery, or Campo Santo, which means sacred ground. The tower is last in line. Together, these buildings make up the Piazza dei Miracoli, which means the Square of Miracles."

"You can say that again," said Ray. "It's a miracle this tower is still standing up."

"No, no, my boy," said Signor Garibaldi,

The Square of Miracles, Pisa, Italy.

shaking his head. "The Leaning Tower is an amazing sight, but it really is not a miracle. Many people over many hundreds of years have done much work to keep this tower standing."

HOW THE LEANING TOWER WAS BUILT

Architects and construction workers started building the Tower of Pisa more than 800 years ago, in 1173. Soon after the work was started, the builders noticed that the south side of the tower was sinking into the swampy soil. Work on the tower went very slowly and carefully after that. Adjustments were made at every stage of construction to try to get the tower to stand up straight. It took almost 200 years to get the whole job finished.

The first architect who worked on the tower was named Bonanno Pisano. The leaders of Pisa chose Bonanno to build the tower because they liked a project he had just finished for them, a great wall that encircled the city.

The tower was supposed to be the **campanile**, or bell tower, for the cathedral. Bonanno also did some work on the cathedral. He designed some beautifully decorated bronze doors to face the bell tower.

When Bonanno laid the **foundation** for the tower, he could make it only about 10 feet deep. A foundation is a stone or concrete base that is placed underground to help hold a building up. The foundation for the Tower of Pisa had to be very shallow because there was a great deal of water in the soil near the ground's surface. In fact, Pisa got its name in about 600 B.C. from a Greek word that means marshy land.

It was well-known in Pisa that the ground was not too solid. But Bonanno hoped for the best and went ahead with his work on the tower.

After the workers had finished building the first level of the tower and the circular balcony above it, they noticed that the floor of the balcony sloped down on the south side. The builders tried to correct this slant by making the columns and arches around the balcony about an inch longer on the south side than on the north.

The construction continued, but so did

the sinking of the soil and the tilting of the tower. At each level of the tower, the builders tried to straighten it with the same method they had used on the first balcony. When they got to the third balcony, they had to make the columns on the south side three inches longer than the columns on the north side.

At this point, the builders seemed to be seized with alarm, and construction on the tower was called off.

"Those builders sound like they had a lot of brains," Ray said. "I'd like to follow their example and call off my trip to the top of the tower. See you guys later!"

"Nonsense, my boy," said Signor Garibaldi as he snagged Ray's arm to stop him from dashing away.

"Yeah. Nonsense, Ray," said Leslie, taking her brother by his other arm.

Signor Garibaldi and Leslie led Ray through the slanted doorway and started up the spiral staircase inside the tower.

"There are 296 steps we must climb to reach the top of the tower," Signor Garibaldi said. "But I think it will not be too difficult for you healthy young people."

DELAYS IN CONSTRUCTION

Climbing the Tower of Pisa is not nearly as difficult as building it was. After Bonanno stopped working on the tower in 1186, many years passed before the construction resumed.

But the tower, in the meantime, had continued to sink. In 1234 an architect named Benenato made a survey of the tower before he started the construction again. He found that the top of the third gallery was now six inches higher on the north side than on the south side.

The same method of trying to straighten the tower by making the columns longer on the south side was used again on the fourth balcony. But Benenato and the builders gave up after that, and construction was stopped again.

A third architect, William of Innsbruck, took charge of the project in 1260. He built the fifth and sixth balconies, and again, he made the columns longer on the south side to try to disguise the lean of the tower. At this

The bell chamber at the top of the Tower of Pisa.

point, the main body of the tower was finished, and all that remained to be built was the bell chamber.

But again, there was a long pause in the building process. Then Tommaso Pisano started building the bell chamber in 1350. The tower was finally finished in 1372, nearly 200 years after Bonanno had laid its foundation.

Before Tommaso started working on the bell chamber, he discovered that the south side of the tower had sunk about eight or nine inches lower than the north side. He tried to correct the tilt by making the stairs and the wall higher on the south side than on the north.

CLIMBING THE TOWER

"It feels like the stairs are slanted right here," Leslie said as she and Ray trudged past the third level behind Signor Garibaldi.

"Yes, yes, you are right again," said Signor Garibaldi. "Perhaps this would be a good place to stop and do a little experiment."

"I hope it's not a hard experiment," said Ray. "All this climbing is starting to make me tired."

"Not to fear," said Signor Garibaldi. "It is a very simple experiment. All you have to do is lean your back against the wall and try to stand up straight."

"Well that certainly sounds easy enough," said Leslie. "Come on, Ray, let's give it a try."

Leslie and Ray turned their backs to the

wall and tried to lean against it. But try as they might, they couldn't lean their whole bodies against the wall without feeling as if they were going to fall flat on their faces.

"Hey! What kind of an experiment is this?" said Ray. "It's impossible to do."

"That is because we are on the north side of the tower," Signor Garibaldi said with a chuckle. "Let's walk around to the south side and try the experiment again. I promise you it will be much easier on the other side."

Just as Signor Garibaldi had promised, Leslie and Ray had no trouble leaning back against the wall on the south side of the tower. But they did have a hard time trying to push themselves away from the wall to stand up straight again.

"Whoa! Now I feel like I'm falling over backwards," said Leslie.

"Correct as usual," said Signor Garibaldi. "You are tilting because the tower is tilting, and you lean in the same direction as the tower does."

"Is that why I feel like I've been leaning sideways the whole way up these steps?" Leslie asked.

"That is exactly why," said Signor Garibaldi.

"I've noticed that, too," said Ray. "You know, this tower is turning out to be kind of fun, after all. It's almost like being on an amusement park ride, isn't it, Leslie?"

"Speak for yourself, Ray," his sister said, clutching her stomach with one hand and holding her forehead with the other. "I think I'm starting to feel a little seasick."

"That is quite a common complaint of visitors who climb the Leaning Tower," said Signor Garibaldi. "The tilt can make you feel a bit woozy if you're not used to it. Perhaps it would help if we stepped outside for some fresh air. Follow me."

Leslie was more than happy to get out of the enclosed stairway. She followed Ray and Signor Garibaldi onto the fourth balcony encircling the tower.

THE LEANING TOWER'S VITAL STATISTICS

"Ah, the **arcades** are truly lovely, aren't they?" Signor Garibaldi said. He took a deep breath and let it out with a long, slow sigh.

"Arcades?" asked Ray. "You mean they have video games and snack bars in the Leaning Tower of Pisa?"

"No, no, my friend," said Signor Garibaldi. "An arcade is a long line of columns and arches around a **gallery**. A gallery is a covered walkway that is open on one side, like this balcony. But I am sure you knew this already."

"Sure, everyone knows what arcades and galleries are," Ray said with a sheepish grin.

There are 15 marble arches, held up by long marble columns, that surround the first gallery of the tower. The next six floors are surrounded by 30 arches each. The eighth level, which is the bell tower, is circled by 16 arches.

The tower is made of 15,000 tons of white marble. The builders tried to make the tower heavier on the north side to keep it from tilting any farther to the south.

On the first level of the tower, the outer wall is 12 feet thick. There are no windows in the outer wall of the tower, but there is a door on each level so visitors can walk outside around the galleries.

The tower is about 50 feet in diameter on the outside and about 24 feet in diameter on the inside.

It is difficult to measure exactly how tall the Leaning Tower is because one side is higher than the other. Most people agree, though, that the highest side is about 179 feet tall.

Scientists at the University of Pisa take measurements of the tower every year on June 21 to see how far it is tilting and sinking. The ground below the tower sinks a little less than a quarter of an inch each year.

The top of the tower leans out about 17 feet beyond the base of the tower. For a long

time, the tower would lean about an eighth of an inch farther every year. But then the rate of the lean started to slow down. Lately, the tower has been leaning about one twentieth of an inch farther every year. If the tower keeps increasing its lean at that rate, it may topple over in about a hundred years.

"That's awful," Ray said. "Why doesn't somebody do something to keep the tower from falling over? Maybe they could prop it up with a big stick or something."

"That's quite an inventive idea," said Signor Garibaldi. "Other people have had some creative ideas about saving the tower, too."

One idea is to drain the water out of the land underneath the tower so the foundation will stop sinking. Another idea is to leave the water in the ground, but to freeze it.

Someone suggested cranking up the tower about six feet off the ground with an enormous jack and then lowering it onto a brand new concrete base. Someone else recommended taking the tower apart and rebuilding it on an entirely new foundation.

Since the 1920s, cement has been injected below the foundation of the tower to try to stabilize it.

THE CURVING
TOWER OF PISA

Because the builders tried to straighten the tower as they went along, each level of the tower leans a little less than the level below it.

"I always thought the tower just leaned in one straight line," said Ray. "I thought it was like a big fat pencil or a giant straw that was stuck in the ground at a tilt."

Signor Garibaldi shook his head. "If the tower really did lean in one straight line, it probably would have fallen over long ago. Remember, the tower started leaning very soon after the architects started building it. The tower leans out quite far near the bottom, but then it starts to curve back a little near the top. The curve helps keep the tower's

center of gravity from leaning too far away from the base of the tower. That is what keeps it from tipping over."

"Wait a minute," Leslie said. "You mean the Leaning Tower of Pisa is also the Curving Tower of Pisa?"

"Yes," said Signor Garibaldi. "That is one way to look at it."

"Hmm, so it isn't straight like a pencil," said Ray. "It's curved like a banana!"

"Yes," said Signor Garibaldi with a little laugh. "I suppose that is one way to look at it, too. But a banana is much more curved than the Leaning Tower is."

DOES THE TOWER
LEAN ON PURPOSE?

"The Leaning Tower of Pisa sure is a complicated building," said Ray. "Hey, I just had an idea. Maybe that architect Bonanno wanted the tower to look like a banana. Maybe the builders made the tower lean on purpose."

"Ah, my friend, you think of everything," said Signor Garibaldi. "But other people also have had this same idea. Some people believe that the architects deliberately built the tower at a slant just to show off."

"Yeah," said Ray. "Those architects must have been really smart if they could build a tower that would tilt but would never fall over. I'll bet they knew what they were doing the whole time. I'll bet they made the tower lean on purpose."

"Well," said Leslie, "maybe the architects just had to be really smart to keep the tower from falling over after it had started leaning. What do you think, Signor Garibaldi? Did the architects make the tower lean on purpose, or was it an accident?"

"The Tower of Pisa is a very beautiful and important building," said Signor Garibaldi. "I cannot believe that the builders would deliberately try to make the tower lean. Why would the architects of such a magnificent building want to put it in danger of toppling down?"

"I guess I hadn't thought of it like that," said Ray.

"Well," said Signor Garibaldi, "this is how I look at it. The architects did everything they could to stop the tower from leaning as they built it. But the swampy soil would not cooperate. The land simply was not solid enough to support the tower. I think the tower would point straight up at the sky if the architects had chosen to build it on a firm piece of ground."

"Then why didn't the architects pick a firmer place to build the tower?" asked Leslie. "Why did they build the tower on such swampy soil?"

"Do you remember how Pisa got its name?" said Signor Garibaldi.

"Oh yeah," said Ray. "The name 'Pisa' comes from a Greek word that means marshy land."

"Exactly, my friend," said Signor Garibaldi. "There is marshy land throughout the whole city of Pisa."

"Then why is the tower the only building in Pisa that is sinking?" asked Ray.

"Ah," said Signor Garibaldi, "you are wrong about that. The Leaning Tower is not the only building in Pisa that is sinking. In fact, the tower is not the only building in this Square of Miracles that is sinking. The cathedral and the baptistery are sinking, too."

"But they don't look like they're sinking," said Leslie.

"No," said Signor Garibaldi. "That is because they are not sinking very much, but still they are sinking. It is much easier to see that the tower is sinking because of the way it leans."

"Why don't the cathedral and the baptistery lean?" asked Ray.

Buildings that are very tall and very slender are more likely to lean than buildings that have a broader base. The cathedral and

The baptistery and cathedral in the Square of Miracles.

the baptistery each cover a much greater area on the ground than the tower does.

The Leaning Tower of Pisa is not the only tower in Pisa that leans. The bell tower at the church of St. Michele dei Scalzi leans. And the bell tower at the church of St. Nicola also leans. The bell tower of St. Mark's cathedral in Venice leans a little, too. But the

Leaning Tower of Pisa in the Square of Miracles has the most noticeable slant.

Ray and Leslie and Signor Garibaldi had walked all the way around the gallery outside the tower. Now they were back at the door that they had come through to get outside.

"Has our stroll in the fresh air helped you to feel better, my young friend?" Signor Garibaldi asked Leslie.

"Oh, yes," Leslie said. "I'm feeling much better now. Why don't we go back inside the tower and take the stairs all the way to the top."

"That is an excellent idea," said Signor Garibaldi. "Let's continue with our climb."

Signor Garibaldi ushered Ray and Leslie back into the tower. They began their journey up the steps again.

ELEVATORS WOULD
BE NICE

"I feel like I'm going up and down, up and down, instead of just going straight up," said Leslie.

"We are going up and down a bit," Signor Garibaldi replied. "But eventually, we will reach the top of the tower."

"It sure would be a lot easier to take an elevator to the top of the tower," said Ray, huffing and puffing.

"Certainly," said Signor Garibaldi, "it would be easier for visitors to ride in an elevator than to climb up 296 steps. But it would not be so easy to build the elevator. It would be difficult, perhaps impossible, to fit an elevator inside the tower. Elevators go straight up and down, but the Leaning Tower does not."

"Oh, yeah," said Ray. "Well, that's too bad about the elevators. How much farther do we have to climb?"

"Not too much farther," said Signor Garibaldi. "We are almost at the top of the tower. In fact, we have just reached the bell chamber now. Come back outside with me and we will look at the bells.

"The Leaning Tower of Pisa was built so the cathedral could have a campanile, or bell tower. The tower has seven bells, and they still ring out over Pisa today."

"Wow! Look at how high up we are," said Ray as he followed Leslie and Signor Garibaldi outside. "This would be a great place to drop a water balloon from. It would soak everybody on the ground."

"I am sure the people on the ground would rather not get soaked by a water balloon," said Signor Garibaldi. "But you are not the first person who has thought of dropping objects off the top of the tower. Pisa's most famous citizen was a scientist named Galileo Galilei. Legend says that he confirmed an important scientific theory by dropping objects off the tower."

GALILEO AND
THE TOWER

Galileo was born in Pisa in 1564, almost 200 years after construction on the Leaning Tower was completed.

One day, Galileo was sitting in the cathedral. There was a large bronze lamp above the pulpit. Galileo saw the lamp swing back and forth. He noticed that it always took the same amount of time for the lamp to make one swing. It didn't matter if the lamp swung over a long distance or a short distance. It always took the same amount of time.

Galileo decided to learn about math. His discovery about the lamp was called the pendulum principle.

"Why did that make him so famous?" asked Leslie.

"Galileo made many great discoveries," said Signor Garibaldi.

"Did he invent the telescope?" Ray asked.

"No," said Signor Garibaldi. "But he was the first person who used a telescope to look at the stars and the moon and the planets.

"Galileo learned all kinds of things with his telescope. He looked at the moon and saw that it was bumpy and uneven. He saw that there are moons around Jupiter. He saw rings around Saturn. He saw that the Milky Way galaxy was a big cluster of stars."

"But what does all of that have to do with the Leaning Tower of Pisa?" Leslie wondered.

"Ah, yes," said Signor Garibaldi. "I almost forgot about the tower. Galileo had a theory that all objects fall at the same speed. Before Galileo, people believed that a heavy object, like a cannonball, would fall faster than a light object, like a rose petal."

Legend has it that Galileo climbed to the top of the Leaning Tower to test his theory. He dropped two balls off the tower at exactly the same time. One of the balls was much heavier than the other, but both balls hit the ground at the very same time. So Galileo proved that his theory was right.

"You mean, if I dropped a feather and a

hammer off the tower, they would hit the ground at the same time?" said Ray.

"Well, yes, they would fall at the same speed," said Signor Garibaldi. "But there might be a problem. A feather is so light that the wind might blow it away. However, if you were on the moon, the experiment would work. The feather and the hammer would hit the ground at the same time."

On one of their trips to the moon, the astronauts had a feather and a hammer with them. They dropped the feather and the hammer on the moon's surface. There is no wind on the moon. The two objects hit the ground at exactly the same time. Galileo's theory was definitely right.

"Just think what would happen if the Leaning Tower of Pisa were on the moon," said Leslie.

"What would happen?" her brother asked.

"Probably nothing," she said, giggling. "The moon's gravity is so weak that it wouldn't pull the tower down any farther. And there's no wind, so the tower would never get blown over. I'll bet the tower could stand on the moon forever and it would never fall down."

A VIEW FROM
THE TOP

"That may be so," said Signor Garibaldi. "But it is so much easier to come to Pisa to see the Leaning Tower than it would be to go to the moon. And Pisa is such a lovely city, besides. Come, let's climb the last few steps to the top of the tower. There we will have a most spectacular view. You are not afraid of heights, are you?"

"Oh, no. I'm not afraid of heights at all," said Leslie. "I can't wait to see the view. Come on, Ray! Let's go to the top!"

Leslie scampered up the steps to the top of the Leaning Tower with Ray and Signor Garibaldi following close behind her.

"Wow!" said Ray as he clambered out onto the top of the tower and looked around

The city of Pisa, showing the Apennine mountain range in the background.

him. "This really is a great view. I feel like I can see forever."

"Yes, we are lucky it is such a clear day," said Signor Garibaldi. "Look over here. Do you see those majestic mountains far away? They belong to the Apennine range. The Apennines span the entire length of Italy."

"Hey! There's a river right down there," said Ray.

"Yes," said Signor Garibaldi. "That is the Arno. It flows between Florence and Pisa."

"Look over here," said Leslie. "I can see the ocean. It's huge!"

"Ah, yes," said Signor Garibaldi. "Pisa is very close to the coast. That water you are looking at is the Ligurian Sea."

"The Ligurian Sea?" said Ray. "I've never heard of it."

"The Ligurian Sea is part of the Mediterranean Sea," said Signor Garibaldi. "You have heard of the Mediterranean Sea, haven't you?"

"I've heard of it," said Leslie.

"Yeah," said Ray, "I've heard of it, too."

"Then you know," said Signor Garibaldi, "that the Mediterranean Sea is surrounded by Europe, Africa and Asia. And you must also know that 'medi' is the Latin word for middle and that 'terra' is the Latin word for earth or land. So 'mediterranean' means in the middle of land."

"Sure," said Ray. "I learned that in geography at school. I just never knew that the Mediterranean Sea had different parts with different names."

"It has several different parts, my friend," said Signor Garibaldi. "The Ligurian Sea lies between the northwest coast of Italy and the island of Corsica, which lies southwest of Pisa."

The Ligurian Sea lies just above the Tyrrhenian Sea. The Tyrrhenian is surrounded by the west coast of Italy and the islands of Corsica, Sardinia and Sicily. The Adriatic Sea and the Ionian Sea on Italy's east coast are also parts of the Mediterranean Sea. The Aegean Sea, between Greece and Turkey, is part of the Mediterranean, too.

PISA'S FORTUNES AT SEA

The sea used to be very important to Pisa, long before the Leaning Tower was built. There were few natural harbors along Italy's central west coast. The Arno River gave Pisa easy access to the sea. That made Pisa a good port city where ships could dock.

Pisa became a major center of trade. Pilgrims on their way from Europe to Jerusalem would stop to rest in Pisa. Merchants from Syria in the Middle East would sail across the Mediterranean to Europe and they would stop in Pisa, too.

Pisan fleets helped defend the southern Italian city of Salerno from attackers in 871. The Pisans also helped to expel Arab forces from the islands Corsica and Sardinia in 1015.

The Pisans sailed all the way down the

Tyrrhenian Sea in 1063 and attacked the city of Palermo on the island of Sicily. They sacked Palermo and captured six big ships that were loaded with valuable goods.

Pisa grew very wealthy from attacking Palermo. The Pisans were eager to show off their new riches. They decided to build a big, new cathedral with the treasures they had taken from Palermo.

"Is that when they built the cathedral here in the Square of Miracles?" asked Leslie.

"Yes, my friend. The very cathedral we are looking at now," said Signor Garibaldi.

"So this cathedral was built with stolen merchandise," Leslie said.

Signor Garibaldi shrugged his shoulders and raised his hands into the air. "I suppose that is one way of looking at it."

The Pisans began to build their cathedral soon after they attacked Palermo in 1063. They used materials from the six ships they had captured, and they also used stones taken from ancient Roman ruins. Today you can still read ancient Roman inscriptions upside down and sideways in the recycled marble blocks of the cathedral's outer walls. The cathedral took about 300 years to complete.

"Why did it take so long to build things back then?" said Ray. "Did they have the same problems with the cathedral that they had with the Leaning Tower?"

"No," said Signor Garibaldi. "The builders did not have problems with the cathedral like they did later with the tower. The cathedral took a long time to finish because the builders kept making it larger for several centuries."

Although the cathedral was not finished yet, Pope Gelasius II **consecrated** it in 1118. The dome of the cathedral was finally finished in about 1380.

In the meantime, the city had grown even more wealthy. The island of Corsica came under Pisa's control in 1077. Pisa took part in the first **crusades** and brought back treasures from Jerusalem. In 1113, Pisa conquered the Balearic Islands near Spain and seized many valuable items.

About a hundred years after work began on the cathedral, the Pisans started to build the baptistery in 1153. Galileo was baptized in Pisa's baptistery in 1565.

Soon after the Pisans started to build the baptistery, they began to build the bell tower in 1173. About a hundred years after that, in

1278, work started on the Campo Santo, or cemetery.

The foundations of the cemetery consist of 53 shiploads of earth that the crusaders brought back from the Hill of Calvary in Jerusalem in 1203. The cemetery was built to hold the tombs that were scattered around the cathedral. It was finally completed in 1463.

By the time the Square of Miracles and its four buildings were completed, Pisa had lost its wealth and power.

In 1284, the nearby town of Genoa defeated Pisa in a battle at sea. Pisa started losing its island colonies. Then, by the 15th century, the mouth of the Arno River had filled with **silt** and blocked Pisa's access to the sea. The city never recovered the wealth and power it once had.

"But how could the Pisans finish all these buildings in the Square of Miracles if they lost all their wealth?" said Leslie.

"It was not easy," said Signor Garibaldi. "The lack of money is one reason these magnificent buildings took so long to finish. But the Pisans had a great sense of pride in their city. They wanted to complete the Square of Miracles and all of its buildings at any cost."

EPILOGUE

"The Square of Miracles does look awfully pretty," Leslie said. "The buildings all seem to go together, and the grass is so beautiful and green."

"Yes," said Signor Garibaldi. "The lawn is one of the things that make the Square of Miracles so special. All of the other cathedral squares in Italy are paved."

"Hey! Look at those people down there on the grass," said Ray.

"What people?" asked Leslie. "All I see is a bunch of little specks."

"Well, I think those two little specks over there are Mom and Dad," Ray said as he pointed at the ground near the back of the cathedral.

"I think you may be right," said Leslie.

"They must be through looking at the paintings and sculptures."

"Good," said Ray. "Maybe they'll take us to get pizza now. All this climbing has been fun, but it's made me even hungrier. Would you like to come with us to eat pizza, Signor Garibaldi?"

"Why, I would love to, my friend," said Signor Garibaldi. "What are we waiting for?"

And with that, the three new friends headed back down the steps to the bottom of the Leaning Tower.

GLOSSARY

ARCADE - A walkway that has an arched roof; a line of arches and their supporting columns.

BAPTISTERY - A building or a part of a church that is used for baptizing.

CAMPANILE - A bell tower that stands apart from any other building.

CATHEDRAL - A large, imposing church.

CENTER OF GRAVITY - The spot around which all of an object's weight is evenly balanced.

CONSECRATE - To declare sacred for religious use.

CRUSADES - Military expeditions that the Christians made from the 11th century to the 13th century to recover the Holy Land from the Moslems.

FOUNDATION - A stone or concrete base that is placed underground to help hold a building up.

GALLERY - A covered walkway that is open at one side or has a roof that is supported by pillars; a long, narrow balcony on the outside of a building

SILT - Fine-grained soil that is carried and laid down by moving water.